DOG BLESSI

by Bob Lovka

illustrations by Setsu Broderick

A COLLECTION OF
POEMS, QUOTES,
FACTS, & MYTHS

BOWTIE™
PRESS

IRVINE, CALIFORNIA

Amy Fox, editor

Nick Clemente, special consultant

Book design and layout by Michele Lanci-Altomare

The cats in this book are alternately referred to as *he* and *she* throughout the book.

Library of Congress Control Number: 2001095702

BowTie™ Press
A Division of BowTie, Inc.
3 Burroughs
Irvine, California 92618
(949) 855-8822

Printed and Bound in Singapore
10 9 8 7 6 5 4 3 2

Dogs are from the human side of heaven (Human Heights, just above Cleveland) where God in his wisdom saw that man and woman weren't going to make it alone and would probably have a heck of a time making it together with all that Mars-Venus communication stuff getting in the way, so he sent the dog to be their partner and to—hopefully—give them some common ground on which to understand each other.

Dogs, being blessed from above, bring blessings to help men and women in this confusing place called—for lack of a better name—earth. Partnering with us since ancient times when a special bond was formed, dogs bless us with their companionship. Dogs bless us with examples of what should be de riguer for humans—loyalty, compassion, friendship, enthusiasm, and nonjudgmental love—but often is not. Dogs work for us, commiserate with us, and communicate with us. Dogs will sometimes even bring the two opposite ends of our us (man and woman) together during a walk in the park, giving us something in common, an easy opening to a conversation, and something both of us can talk about and understand...finally.

This splendid little book celebrates all the blessing-giving canines who share this world with us. From affenpinschers and Afghan hounds to whippets and Yorkshire terriers, their blessed nature helps us make it together.

The Puppy's Home Recipe

Take one house
Fill it with four little legs, supporting a bundle of fur
Mix in
One tiny tail (of wagging variety)
A dose of milky-scented breath (warmed)
Toss in a near-mouthful of prickly-pincher teeth
And what you have is a home.

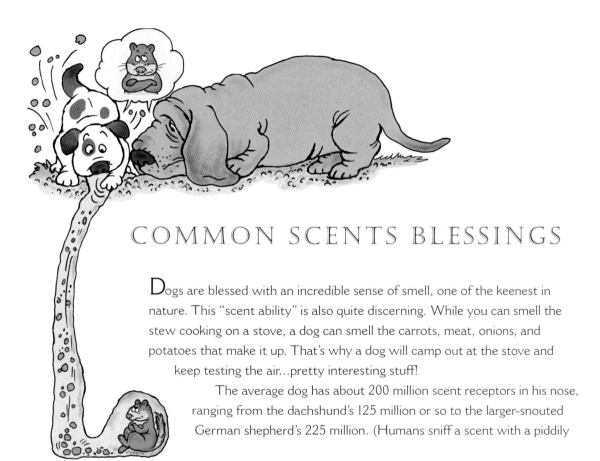

COMMON SCENTS BLESSINGS

Dogs are blessed with an incredible sense of smell, one of the keenest in nature. This "scent ability" is also quite discerning. While you can smell the stew cooking on a stove, a dog can smell the carrots, meat, onions, and potatoes that make it up. That's why a dog will camp out at the stove and keep testing the air...pretty interesting stuff!

The average dog has about 200 million scent receptors in his nose, ranging from the dachshund's 125 million or so to the larger-snouted German shepherd's 225 million. (Humans sniff a scent with a piddily

5 million receptor cells.) Curiously, it has been shown that a canine's color has a direct effect on his ability to smell things, with dogs of a darker color catching things better than their lighter-colored brothers and sisters.

Dogs take in smells from scenting glands on the roof of their mouth. Basset hounds, bloodhounds, and beagles are among the major scent hounds that exhibit an even greater talent for sniffing.

Humans are blessed to have a dog's acute sense of smell at their disposal. Dogs and their noses have played detective roles for police and fire departments, the military, and in search and rescue operations. Dogs can effectively sniff out bombs, and have proven to be the fastest and most efficient tools in mine-clearing efforts. They can lead a search for lost children, aid in finding victims buried after earthquakes and natural disasters, and can track down escaped criminals—their sense of smell is so powerful that with training a dog can pick out a particular human footprint weeks after being imprinted in the ground. Dogs also act as key sleuths in arson investigations.

Scientists are also discovering a dog's blessing of "scenta-mentality." In humans, many biochemical processes trigger mood swings. These are from pheromone/hormone secretions that can be detected as scents, or odors. Doctors and researchers are attempting to identify schizophrenia in humans by training dogs to detect the pheromones associated with that disorder. Dogs have been used to detect the presence of human skin cancer, and it appears that dogs can sniff out emotions ranging from the anxious to the serene. Dogs seem to know when their owners need a lift and can detect stress. Along with reading an owner's visual and verbal attitude, a dog gets an uncanny read of the emotional state. A dog is truly an empathetic friend.

A dog's "scent ability" lends to his own amusement. By making up simple games such as finding a toy or treat, you can create playtime that develops your dog's sense of smell. A new chew or treat wrapped in a paper bag, placed inside a larger bag, and left on the floor usually results in a fun hunt, sniff, and tear-open triumph. Scent activities, games, or getting involved with competitive tracking groups tend to build a dog's confidence and sense of security. The dog gets to use his special scentability to the fullest and you get to partake in the activities—everyone is blessed!

Walk Time

Front Paws
reach up to my legs
stretched between ottoman and chair.

Eye Contact
large
bright
eager and expectant

Then…
A half-whimpered bark.
A run across rugs to the front door
A look back…Come On!

Walk time is here.

BLESSED FROM
THE BEGINNING

A Native American legend holds that at one time the Great Spirit decided to divide the world in two, creating a world of animals and a world of people. Gathering all of earth's inhabitants, he then drew a line in the dirt across a great plain, placing mankind on one side and the animals on the other. The Spirit then began to open a great crevice in the earth along the line, but as it widened, separating the two worlds forever, the dog leapt over the chasm and joined the world of humans choosing them as rightful partner.

Dog. A kind of additional or subsidiary Deity designed to catch the overflow and surplus of the world's worship.

—AMBROSE BIERCE

A GUIDE TO UNDERSTANDING BASIC DOG COMMUNICATIONS

ACT:

Pulling the blankets off your bed in the morning

Standing still and staring at the doggy dish

Walking to the stove and sniffing the air

Walking away from the doggy dish to sit alertly and obediently by your side at the dinner table

Happily dropping a ball, stick, or flying disk at your feet

MEANING:

I want breakfast!

I need food!

I need YOUR food!

Please pass the people food.

Trade you this for food!

TALK TO ME

It's a blessing to be able to communicate and interact with others. Responding to others, being responded to, and forming a link between yourself and someone else is a validation of who you are and gives you a comforting feeling that you're not isolated in some big scary world. Communicating leads to familiarity, and familiarity gives you a sense of security.

People need people, but there's a special blessing in communicating across species with the other living beings on the planet. Dogs are blessed with a great set of communicative talents! Not only do they vocalize but canine body language also twists and turns out a vocabulary of its own.

A dog's tail is a major tool in canine linguistics. Dogs inherited this from their ancestor the wolf, who used her tail to express a wide range of communiqués to other wolves. In

wolves, the tail held upright signals, *I'm number one* in the game of pack dominance. Add a slight upward curve and it's usually an exclamation point saying, *I'm warning you...don't even try!* A twitching tail, a tail tucked under, and the loosely hanging *Laid-back-and-lovin'-it* tail all impart communications as to what's going on in a dog's world. Today's proud pup has kept most of these signals and modified others to reflect her own lifestyle. The upraised tail of a dog whose only other pack member is you usually is a sign that she's happy and that all is well with whatever the two of you are doing.

Dogs also bless people with a lot of "talk." A bark can mean a variety of things depending on the circumstances: the excitement of play, the frustration of you not doing something the dog wants you to do (such as feeding or taking a walk), or just be the result of plain boredom. It's time for you to talk back! A barking and panting combination is heavy-duty playfulness.

Some dogs howl just for the fun of it, but howling, at least in the predomesticated days, was employed by dogs to communicate over distances to locate other dogs. A forlorn howl is a call indicating loneliness—a cry of, *Is anybody out there?* Sudden pain or a startled surprise brings a yelp, while longer-lasting pain can cause a whimper. Whimpering can also mean anxiety or a fearful submission. Time for a reassuring pep (or pup) talk!

A dog's distinctive *You-better-run-the-other-way* growl is a show of aggression. When accompanied by some short barks it's usually a matter of possession, as in *I'm guarding this bone and that's that!* Under such circumstances, the dog may need a good talking to!

Study a dog with her peers and you'll get a glimpse into a whole world of canine pecking orders, social rules, and salutations. Making direct eye contact could mean the dog is feeling confident, while an averted gaze signals a deference to another dog. Relaxed ears show calmness, while erect ears signal the dog is alert and interested. Ears pricking up and forward show assertiveness and possibly a challenge. The dog receiving these signals might lay back his ears, indicating worry or fear.

Dogs paw the ground as an appeasing move toward friendliness, lick another dog's face in deference, or extend a joyous invitation to play by hunkering down and bowing with rump raised, front legs extended, and tail wagging furiously. Who could resist?

For dogs, rubbing up or leaning against a new acquaintance is a sign of friendliness and a gesture of companion-ship. Don't try this at home. In the human world, it's a sign for a harassment suit.

Evolution

Grandpa's dog would hunt and fish,
Retrieving catch and prey.
He'd bring in the mail,
Lug magazines,
Even tote packages along the way.

Dad's dog was suburban.
He loved to fetch and play.
He'd even meet the paperboy
To bring the news in every day.

My dog is of the Millennium.
There is nothing he'll go get.
And instead of bringing in the news
He boots up the Internet!

For some of his lofty communications, the great Odin, god of Norse legend, used two dogs as messengers.

—CANINE MYTHOLOGY

Near this spot are deposited the
remains of one who possessed
Beauty without vanity,
Strength without Insolence,
Courage without Ferocity,
and all the Virtues of Man
without his Vices.
This praise, which would have
unmeaning Flattery, if inscribed
over human ashes, is but a just
Tribute to the Memory of
BOATSWAIN, a Dog.

—JOHN CAM HOBHOUSE FOR AN INSCRIPTION
ON THE MONUMENT RAISED FOR LORD BYRON'S DOG

A BLESSED
BONDING

The bond between dog and person is a unique, mutually beneficial interspecies relationship. It's a very special way that dogs bless us. Since prehistoric times, dogs have been our significant others in the human world.

A special bond has developed between humans and dogs that goes back to the Stone Age. Cave drawings depict early dog—more of a wolf—as a hunting companion. Man and wolf began hunting together five thousand years before the concept of planting and harvesting food took root in the mind of Man (or maybe it was wolf-dog who came up with the idea).

Early Man, the Cro-Magnon, made an ideal teammate for the wolf/dog when hunting because both used the same strategy: hunt in packs or groups with one hunter flushing out the prey while others move in for the kill, then split the proceeds.

A dog has the soul of a philosopher

—PLATO

 While the adult dogs were off hunting with the good ol' Magnons, it is conceivable that the puppies were left at "home sweet cave" with the women and children. Puppies became the first companion animals—the invention of the pet!

Besides being hunting companions, dogs also lent their barking and howling talents as guard dogs, warning the pack that the community boundaries were being trespassed by another clan. Both human and canine have a territorial imperative.

Dogs (and wolves) are pack animals and readily identify with the group concept. Like humans, dogs derive companionship, security, protection, and identity from their family pack. That could be part of the reason for the bond between us. For better or worse, humans and dogs developed civilization together, and the partnership continues today.

Dogs were even cosmonauts in early space programs.

The bond between dog and humans is a mutually beneficial interspecies relationship that is unique. It's a very special way that dogs bless us.

The best thing about a man is his dog.

—FRENCH PROVERB

The Blessed Dream
of Favored Things

Dishfuls of food
and a beef-basted chew
A flower bed to dig in
that won't upset you

A mailman
a meter reader
and a stranger to bark at
Chasing a car
a squirrel
and that ornery cat

A forest of trees
made for lifting a leg
A handful of treats
without having to beg
The freedom to sniff
and not get pulled away
Head petting and back scratching
all through the day.

THE BLESSINGS OF LAUGHTER

Dogs are the clowns of the pet populace.

Dogs are uninhibited enough to not give a darn about how foolish they look while chasing their own tails, giving us a lesson in not taking ourselves too seriously.

While cats will abruptly change demeanor and deny any clumsy move they make, dogs relish the idea of pratfalls, mistakes, and shtick. Dogs are always ready to give you the goofiest facial expressions on the planet just so you'll play with them! And, their enthusiastic barks are saying, *Throw the ball; throw the stick; heck, throw ANYTHING, or just PRETEND to and I'll be tripping and tumbling after it like you wouldn't believe! Do it! Do it! Do it!*

Self-conscious? Not a chance. Dogs allow you to be yourself in all your shambles and screwups, never once pulling a superiority act and making you feel foolish. They're too busy having fun acting foolish themselves!

Dogs relish slippery linoleum floors to skid across in pursuit of dinner, peanut butter on their tongues so they lick like crazy and crack you up, and Mother Nature's number one fun soil: mud! Sand counts for big time kicks, too. Take a dog to the beach and his Marx

Brothers behavior will have him clomping into the waves and storming back to you shaking, sand and sea water to and fro, up and down, in and out, and everywhere, while chewing the most god-awful clump of kelp that Neptune ever put in the sea. Fun stuff and totally unrestrained!

If you're going to cut loose, be spontaneous, and have a laugh with a species other than your own, it will more than likely be with a dog. "Doggy Dignity" is always accompanied by a smirk, just to let you know that there is no such thing. Canines bring blessings wrapped in laughter.

Every Day Is a Dog's Holiday

Every day is New Year's Day
to celebrate through the year.
Every day is Valentine's Day
filled with love and frolicking good cheer.
No matter the time of season
there's a holiday dogs see.
Every day is Arbor Day
celebrated by sniffing every tree!

Dogs spring over meadows
Graduating to the green
with summery dispositions
that last through fall's air, crisp and clean.
A dog's love knows no winter.
Their Thanksgiving is thanking you.
And the Christmas gifts dogs bring
is loyalty, tried and true.

THE EIGHT DOGGY BEATITUDES

1. Blessed are the cocker spaniels and beagles, for theirs is the kingdom of doggy heaven.

2. Blessed are the humble dachshunds, for they shall possess the low-lying land.

3. Blessed are the mournful-looking bassets, bulldogs, and bloodhounds, for they shall be comforted.

4. Blessed are the hyperactive Jack Russell terriers, who hunger and thirst constantly, for they shall have their fill.

5. Blessed are the merciful Saint Bernards, for they shall obtain mercy.

6. Blessed are the clean little poodles, Pomeranians, and Pekingese, for they shall see the Master's bed.

7. Blessed are the peaceful golden retrievers, for they shall be called the canines of gentleness.

8. Blessed are the mutts that suffer and are overlooked for human friendship, for theirs is the joy of the dinner dish and stuffed pillows of paradise.

SIX LITTLE DOG BLESSINGS YOU PROBABLY TAKE FOR GRANTED

1. The cold, wet nose alarm clock in the morning

2. The traipsing to be with you for no reason at all

3. Little tickling foot licks

4. The feel of the coat and the sound of the breathing

5. Being there…no matter what happens

6. Coming back for more play, more love, or more attention even after you've been bad-tempered.

Canis Nongossipus

A reason for popularity so far-flung
is that a dog wags his tail
instead of his tongue!

They are better than human beings because they know but do not tell.

—EMILY DICKINSON

"FOO DOG" BLESSINGS

People often ask why I blessed my pseudo–mixed-breed dog (half Lhasa apso, half Tasmanian devil—I've got the scars to prove it) with the name Foon. I've wondered that myself, but finally realized that Foon, being a Lhasa apso (at least part of the time), is of Far Eastern origin like the legendary foo dogs, or dogs of fo!

Foo dogs are actually small, decoratively carved, pug-looking lions that represent the guardian lion for the Buddha (fo in Chinese). Thus, they are believed to bring good luck and act as guardians over the entrance to temples and tombs, discouraging wrongdoers and evil spirits from entering. Unlike my "Foo," these Buddhist lion-dogs maintain peace and tranquility over the areas they guard.

Foo dogs are usually depicted in pairs with one of the dogs' paws atop a ball or a sphere and sometimes shown with a baby fo. They can be traced back to the art of the Han dynasty (207 B.C. to 220 A.D.) but then seem to disappear from record, only to show up again during the Tang dynasty around 600 A.D. Maybe they were hiding out with Lhasas for four hundred years.

So far be it that Foon is a frivolous or nonsense name! Steeped in history and legend, Foon is a righteous, blessed name associated with Buddha himself. Besides, with that short body, blonde coat, and all that hair flopping over her eyes, my dog just looks like she should be called Foon.

BLESSINGS OF SIGHT AND SOUND

Dogs are a pretty pliable lot. They're partners with us, and because of their ingrained work ethic, dogs respond to training and accept work that we put before them. Try that with a cat, iguana, porcupine, or nearly any other animal, and you'll be either ignored or looked at as if you're crazy for asking!

Dogs can be trained to take on the duties of being working partners to us as service dogs. Service dogs are specially trained to act as direct human helpers, making life better for people. They can be eyes for the blind and ears for the hearing impaired.

Using guide dogs for the blind dates back to 79 A.D. when Pompeii was destroyed.

An art fresco discovered in Pompeii depicts a man brandishing a staff while being led by a dog. Chinese art of the thirteenth century and European literature from the fourteenth century contain references to dogs guiding the blind. The first American partnership of a seeing-eye dog and a blind person is believed to have formed in 1928, modeled after European efforts.

Guide dogs bless their owners with mobility comparable to that enjoyed by the average-sighted person. Trained not only to be command-takers, guide dogs are actually taught to be thinkers and to take initiative!

They are not only trained to avoid traffic and obstacles but also to learn "intelligent disobedience," refusing to move into the path of oncoming vehicles in spite of being commanded to do so. Good thinking! These canine aids move on when safety dictates, signal their owners by stopping at curbs and stairs, and bark to alert other pedestrians as to the situation at hand.

Hearing dogs are trained to aid the deaf and hearing impaired. They distinguish sounds and then alert their partner by running back and forth between the partner and the sound, or by physically leading the deaf partner to the sound source. The dog alerts his companion to specific sounds such as the buzz of a smoke alarm; the ring of an alarm clock, telephone, or timer; the cry of a baby; the knock at a door; sirens; the scurrying of a mouse in the pantry; or whatever might go bump in the night. Hearing dogs also act as safety guardians, signaling the presence of another person nearby. Regardless of the sound or action, a hearing dog is custom-trained to match the specific lifestyle of his partner.

Although it's a large responsibility, small to medium mixed breeds make up the majority of hearing dogs. Training is generally initiated when puppies are six months to a year old. Some are donated to a training program by independent dog breeders, others are bred by the service organizations, and others are acquired from animal shelters, receiving the blessing of a home in return for the blessings they will soon be giving.

Service dogs also bless their partners with joys and benefits. Hearing- or sight-impaired individuals often feel isolated from the world at large. The big world can become a very small place without the visual and auditory faculties presenting the framework. A guide dog or a hearing dog opens up the world for impaired individuals, allowing them to socialize more effectively and with less stress. Service dog owners tend to feel more comfortable and independent in interactive situations. This leads to feelings of self-confidence, an increase in self-esteem, and more effective functioning outside the home. What miraculous blessings!

BLESSINGS OF ASSISTANCE

Dogs have become the eyes and ears for millions of people, but they also act as the arms and legs of people with physical or mental disabilities.

These versatile, reliable, personal assistants—butlers and valets in fur—are truly remarkable. They have been trained to open doors, press elevator buttons, turn light switches on and off, retrieve dropped objects, and even take specific items off grocery shelves. They can handily pull a wheelchair or carry a person's bag or purse. Can you name another animal (including humans) who will do all that for you and keep asking to do more?

Dogs become extensions of people in regard to performing physical tasks. Assistance dogs can be custom-trained to assist their handler's specific lifestyle and need: mobile assistant dogs specialize in carrying things like backpacks and purses, pulling a wheelchair, picking up things that fall to the floor, opening and closing doors, and helping owners get dressed. They can even transfer laundry into and out of a washer and dryer! And like the helpful angels they are, they never ask for a raise. Walkers are adept at acting as a counter-balance to keep their partners on an even keel, help lead them past objects, and help them up from a fall or a seated position.

Some dogs are blessed with an unexplainable alert-and-response ability. Many dogs demonstrate the uncanny sensitivity to warn their owners of an oncoming seizure, enabling people to prepare for the attack and situate themselves safely. The dog will then stay with the person for support or get help. They can also be taught to call 911 by hitting an automatic dial button on a telephone and then bark into the speaker when the emergency call is picked up.

The independence that these special dogs bring is also a great psychological blessing to their owners. No matter the physical disability, a person is freed from relying on random assistance from another person, whether it's to pick up the dropped pencil, carry a package home, or act as a stopgap from falling. Assistance dogs also act as a buffer in crowds and are great navigators, allowing an owner easier movement through hordes of people.

These dog blessings make it possible for a person to act without having to plan each and every step, thereby affording a person the freedom to pursue goals and spend more time on the good things in life. Dogs can bring the blessing of being able to fully participate in life no matter what the outward circumstances may be. It's the greatest canine blessing of all!

Pets and Their People

It seems to me
that if you look, you'll see
a most discernible similarity
between dogs and their people
and those people to their pets
to the point of utmost hilarity!

From body types to hair styles
and from faces dour to sour to sweet
we choose the dog
who shares our visage
becomes our twin
forming an image in repeat!

Now there's no harm in the practice
at least from the human point of view
but questions arise
as you might surmise....

Does the dog really *want to look*
like you?

SEVEN BLESSINGS DOGS
APPLY TO DAILY LIFE

1. Greeting a loved one with glee

2. Walking with a special someone

3. Running, romping, and playing in the
    middle of the day

4. Enjoying the benefits of a hearty appetite

5. Being touched by someone near and dear

6. Chewing on the simple pleasures of today
    instead of grousing about tomorrow

7. Taking every opportunity to breathe
    the air and relish the wind in your face

*History is more
full of examples
of the fidelity
of dogs than
of friends.*

—ALEXANDER POPE

Blessedly Simple Daily Advice from Dogs Who Know

*If you simply do
what you need to do
at the time it needs to be done
You'll avoid the stress
that makes life a mess
and still have time for some fun!*

SUPERNATURAL BLESSINGS

The wolf, and especially the coyote among Pueblo tribes, play prominent roles in the many Native American tribe stories about creation and sacred traditions.

The dog plays a most blessed role in the creation of the Chipewyan people. As the story goes, a primordial woman lived alone in a cave. One night, a spirit in the shape of a dog crept into the cave and lay close beside her. As he did so, his limbs grew humanlike, his skin became smooth, and his features transformed into those of a handsome young man. Nine months later, a baby was born. This baby was the first Chipewyan. Ever since, the dog has merited special respect from the Chipewyan people.

The spirits of dogs bless the Hopi and Zuni. Among these tribes, religion plays a preeminent role in everyday life. At the core of the religion are the helpful kachinas, masked impersonators infused with ancestral spirits. The kachina is the spiritual counterpart of the animal, ancestor, or plant it impersonates—a divine essence. The dog kachina is the ancestral spirit aiding the Hopi in the hunt.

The unbreakable connection between dogs and humans is supernatural, influential, and timeless.

THE FIRST CHIPEWYAN

COMPANIONS,
EVEN IN THE STARS

The constellation Canis Major (the great dog) follows his master, the constellation Orion (the hunter), as Orion crosses the night sky. Sirius, the dog star, is the brightest star in the heavens and is located on the shoulder of Canis Major, lighting the way for the hunt.

PLAYFUL MUSICAL BLESSINGS

Italian composer Gioacchino Rossini who wrote the operas *The Barber of Seville* and *William Tell* was known for his playfulness, comic invention, tricks, and teasing. No wonder he was fond of dogs! Once when asked what he was composing, Rossini replied that he was working on a little composition for his dog's birthday, a tribute he claimed to make every year! Perhaps he was only half-kidding. Among the over 150 piano pieces, songs, and ensembles that comprise the work called *Sins of Old Age,* Rossini had earmarked such

pieces as "Love Songs To My Dog," What a blessed arrangement! The man who once said he could set a laundry list to music surely could write the definitive dog love song.

Frederic Chopin was also influenced by a dog's playfulness, and in his case, the result was the famous "Minute Waltz" (Waltz no. 6 in D-flat, op. 64, no. 1). As the story goes, George Sand had a rambunctious little dog who tirelessly chased his tail around and around in circles. So amused was Chopin that he improvised the "Minute Waltz" around the antics of the dog! Actually, the piece has been more accurately called "The Little Dog Waltz." These colorful nicknames were acquired through popular reference to them, as Chopin didn't title his compositions. The great composer never intended the piece to be played in one minute (the proper duration is about two minutes). The word "minute," referring to diminutive, small, or short, became confused with "minute." The title was meant to describe the score, not the playing time. Only a dog could bless one piece of music with so many interpretations!

My little old dog: A heart-beat at my feet.

—EDITH WHARTEN
"A LYRICAL EPIGRAM"

Elizabeth Barrett Browning's
Other Sonnet (to Her Dog)

How have you changed me? Let me count the ways....
You have changed me to the depth, breadth, and height
My arms can reach
To keep the garbage, my shoes, and dinner out of your reach.
You have changed the way I awaken
Not by sun and alarm, but by sniff and lick.
You have changed me freely, as I am softhearted
You have changed me purely, as now I acquire only life's basics:
Leashes, Treats, and Pooper-Scooper.
Yet, I love thee with a love I seem to lose
And despite what I would choose
You have changed me with the doggy breath, smiles, and fetches
Missing from all my life.
You have changed a part of everything...however, I still love you.

THE DO-AS-I-DO GUIDE
TO LIVING A DOG'S LIFE

1. Awake without complaining over chronic aches and pains.

2. Set a steady course, and don't howl and yowl over your problems to everybody else.

3. Be grateful food is there, even if it's about the same thing every day.

4. Take correction and direction to learn from your mistake—then don't hound yourself about it.

5. Be true to all around you; there's no good in deceit and lies.

6. Don't take it personally if someone is too busy, too bothered, or too stupid to give you some quality time.

7. Relax without cigarettes and alcohol. Sleep without pills.

8. Be comfortable wherever you lie down.

BLESSINGS OF COURAGE AND HEROISM

Our blessed partner, the dog, will accompany us anywhere, even into war. War dogs protect the soldiers they serve with, displaying valiant courage by going great lengths to save their human cohorts from the tragedies of combat. The bond between soldier and war dog is one of loyalty, love, and mutual survival. America saw thousands of dogs serving their country throughout World War II, the Korean War, the Vietnam War, and Desert Storm. These canine heroes

were scouts, trackers, and sentries who were trained in lifesaving skills to detect trip wires and mine tunnels, discover weapons and caches, and recognize booby traps. They warned troops of ambushes and saved lives by literally dragging soldiers to safety.

It is estimated that war dogs prevented ten thousand casualties in the Vietnam War alone. They were the only true blessings on a cursed battlefield. Yet for all their loyalty and sacrifice, less than two hundred of these valiant dogs returned home after the Vietnam War. Being heartlessly designated "surplus armaments," most were euthanized or left behind by military and government officials.

The everyday soldiers who had served on the front lines with these dogs, and who in many cases owe their lives to them, did not forget them. After the dogs were denied official recognition, military commendation, or memorial placing, GIs took up the cause to honor these heroes.

Through dedicated work, a documentary film, and various fundraising, two war dog memorials were created to commemorate the acts of heroism performed by war dogs, fostering a national awareness of the significant role canines play in military history.

The first memorial was dedicated on President's Day 2000 at March Field Air Museum in Riverside, California, in a touching ceremony attended by the public and groups of veterans, military, and law enforcement. It included a keynote speech by a California Supreme Court Justice. A second memorial, also heavily attended, was held in October 2000 at the National Infantry Museum in Fort Benning, Georgia.

Aesthetically, the War Dog Memorial is an impressive sculpture. World-renowned artist A. Thomas Schomberg's tribute depicts a soldier and his dog entering a combat zone together, looking into fields of impending danger. This emotional work illuminates the partnership, protection, sacrifice, and love between soldier and dog. The sites are open to the public year-round.

Aiding soldiers by their courage, loyalty, and love, war dogs are the epitome of the special bond between humankind and canine. The inscription on the War Dog Memorial describes what their handlers felt about these special comrades, "They protected us on the field of battle. They watch over our eternal rest. We are grateful."

If a man lived up to the reputation of a dog, he would be a saint.

—ZANZIBARIAN PROVERB

A CANINE'S SELECTIVE INTERPRETATION

Dogs are blessed with a phenomenal understanding of human language. However, being the wise beings (some would say "wise guy") they are, dogs reserve the right to *interpret* human language in a way that's most beneficial to themselves. This "selective interpretation" of your greetings, conversations, commands, requests, or scoldings aimed at them has served dogs well throughout their glorious history and has been passed down from generation to canine generation.

After years of exhaustive research, I have finally cracked the interpretation code that dogs employ in understanding humans. You may think you are communicating clearly with your dog—and you probably are—but that's no guarantee that the dog will do what you expect him to do. It's all a matter of a canine's selective interpretation. Keep this in mind when using key words or phrases when speaking to your dog. You can avoid a lot of frustration by understanding how your words are being translated by the canine mind.

HUMAN KEY WORDS:

"Hi (dog's name)!"

"Bath time!"

"I am so exhausted!" or
"My feet are killing me."

"Outside"

"GET DOWN OFF THE BED NOW!"

CANINE INTERPRETATION:

Great! It's time to eat!

*Here we go with his spilling water all over the place,
slipping on soap, yelling, and crying game.
Why do they like that? Whatever…
let's play it.*

Yay! Walk time!

Lie down

*Since there is
no known canine
interpretation for this
configuration of words most
dogs will simply ignore them.*

TEN THINGS DOGS KEEP TRYING TO TELL US

1. Silly is better than self-conscious.

2. It's more fun to play it than watch it.

3. There is much to be said for going barefoot.

4. Take time to be fascinated by something…even a moving line of ants.

5. It doesn't have to be a designer dog dish for the food to taste good.

6. Anything has the potential to be a toy.

7. Sometimes you've got to splash in the puddles.

8. Don't do anything halfway.

9. Kisses are meant to be REALLY BIG!

10. A little love makes a big difference.

I love a dog.
He does nothing
for political reasons.

—WILL ROGERS

The Very Thoughtful Dog's Bedtime Blessing

Now I lay me down to sleep
then onto your bed I'll faithfully creep
A thoughtful sentry at your feet
guarding your dreams, ensuring they're sweet!
Now all I want is what is fair, but I'm down here and you're way up there!
Since I can't let my protection slip
I'd better move up by your hip.
There, that's better. But are you calling me?
That might be snoring; I'd better go see.

Ah, here we are…a vacant place.
My head can fit right by your face!
I admit this may sound pretty nice
actually, it's a sacrifice.
There's my wake-up call with the
morning sun
But that's okay,
Don't thank me,
A dog's work is never done.

Little Blessings from the Last Litter

Tumbling and bumbling as they bound toward you,
Mouths always searching for something to chew.
There's licking and lapping
Some squeaks and a yip.
Little needle teeth that don't bite, but nip.
Tails that stick up:
Something to chase?
Now they're spreading your laundry
All over the place!
They're skidding across waxed kitchen floors
Bopping headfirst into cabinet doors.
It's the puppy brigade!
They're active and cute
They're silly, they're fun.
But you're going to go crazy
If you keep more than one!
(Well…maybe two?)

When the Man waked up he said, "What is Wild Dog doing here?" And the Woman said, "His name is not Wild Dog any more, but the First Friend, because he will be our friend for always and always and always."

—RUDYARD KIPLING, "THE CAT THAT WALKED BY HIMSELF" IN *JUST SO STORIES*

COHORTS, COMPANIONS, AND THERAPEUTIC FRIENDS

Julius Caesar kept two greyhounds. Queen Victoria was accompanied by her Pomeranians. Winston Churchill's bulldog became a symbol of Britain's unconquerable spirit during World War II. Price Charles and Princess Diana shared time with their Jack Russell terrier. Dogs have provided companionship to world leaders, kings, and potentates throughout history.

Fittingly, America's premier founding father George Washington was a dog lover. As a dog breeder, Washington crossed staghounds given to him by the Marquis de Lafayette with smaller breeds of black and tan Virginia hounds and is credited with founding the American foxhound breed.

Washington also understood the special relationship between an owner and his dog. During the War of Independence a lost, hungry, but well-bred hound wandered into Washington's battle camp. The general soon recognized him as the dog belonging to British commander Richard Howe. Setting aside the differences of war and tuning in to something more universal, Washington returned the dog to Howe's camp under a white flag. Leave it to a dog to provide a cease-fire during a war!

A dog's companionship and devotion are woven into the fabric of our human world. The way dogs have blessed the movers and shakers of history is the same way they've blessed the everyman living next door. Perhaps the most vivid example of the devotion and companionship dogs bring to us is found in the true story of Greyfriars Bobby.

Bobby was a Skye terrier belonging to John Gray, a policeman in Edinburgh, Scotland. In 1858, Gray died and was buried in the old Greyfriars Kirk (churchyard). His largely untended grave had few mourners and infrequent visitors, except for one: his devoted dog, Bobby, who for fourteen years kept constant watch over his master's grave. Despite being repeatedly driven away in the early weeks following Gray's death, Bobby always returned to his vigil and soon won the admiration of the cemetery caretaker and the townspeople— some of whom tried to take Bobby in, only to find him relentless in returning to the grave. Bobby became a local legend, and the lord provost of the city granted Bobby the freedom to roam Edinburgh unattended by a human. Bobby faithfully guarded his companion and master until his own passing in 1872 and was buried next to him at Greyfriars.

So touched by this story of canine companionship, a Scottish baroness commissioned a bronze statue of the devoted dog to be erected in the churchyard. Today, it is one of the most photographed statues in all of Scotland, standing near the crest of Candlemaker Row at the entrance of the churchyard gates.

The blessing of a dog's special companionship even extends into modern medical and psychological therapies. Humans have an affinity with dogs, which allows dogs to be of great benefit in therapy. Companion dogs are used to assist in therapy in hospitals, nursing homes, prisons, psychiatric institutions, schools in alcohol and drug treatment centers, and for autistic children.

If there are no dogs in heaven, then when I die I want to go where they went.

—UNKNOWN

The first idea for using dogs in therapy in the United States came in 1919 when then Secretary of the Interior, F. K. Lang, touted dogs as companions for patients in psychiatric hospitals. Since then it has been well documented in studies that the presence of dogs is both physically and psychologically beneficial to patients of all ages. Pets, dogs in particular, are especially effective therapeutically for the elderly and the infirmed who are cut off from regular human interactions. Dog visitation programs have helped people feel less lonely and depressed. It has been observed that patients become more active and responsive during and after dog visits to their hospital room and convalescent home.

In speech therapy, a dog often will act as encouragement for patients who have stopped speaking, acting as a catalyst for people to issue commands and to verbally respond to the dog's attention. Dogs also aid in limited physical therapy. Patients can exercise and rebuild muscles by throwing a ball, stretching and turning to pet a dog, and walking a dog.

Companion therapy dogs seem to connect to people on a deep level. The dogs allow people to share their thoughts, feelings, and memories. A dog companion can also bless the terminally ill with a welcomed distraction from pain and fear, offer something to look forward to, and serve as a break from the normal routine.

Dog companionship also blesses us with emotional support and healing. There is comfort in having someone there for us in times of sadness or bereavement. In our private hours, we will open up our heart and emotions to a nonjudgmental dog in lieu of burdening another human with our pain. Anything can be said to a dog without fear of reprisal or shame.

While not a replacement for human affection, companionship, or concern, dogs nevertheless provide a welcome substitute for the companionship and contact that we all need. Dogs are blessedly there for us.

A dog is man's best friend, and vice versa.

—ANONYMOUS

'Tis sweet to hear the watch-dog's honest bark
Bay deep-mouthed welcome as we draw near home;
'Tis sweet to know there is an eye will mark
Our coming, and look brighter when we come.

—LORD BYRON

A BLESSING RETURNED... DOG RESCUE

For all that dogs do for us, there is a major blessing we can provide for them: homes.

Over 10 million dogs, including approximately 2 million purebreds, are euthanized in the United States every year simply for lack of a home. To combat the staggering numbers, thousands of rescue groups nationwide work tirelessly to find homes and provide safety for these innocent best friends who have nowhere to go. Private rescue and shelter groups exist in every community and state. There are a variety of ways anyone can help to return a blessing to a dog that sorely needs one.

By volunteering your time and your heart, you can make a difference. Rescue groups are always in need of people to answer phones, follow up on calls, feed orphaned pets, and help with the necessary clean up. On a direct level, you can foster a pet, providing a temporary home while permanent owners are being found.

Many organizations can cover the food, medical costs, and other necessities for the fostered dog. All you need to supply is your love. If you have neither the place to foster a dog nor the time to volunteer, rescue organizations are in constant need of donations to keep operating. Most are tax deductible charities so your monetary blessing will in turn give you a blessing (or a reprieve) from Uncle Sam at tax time.

Of course, attacking the problem on the front end by spaying or neutering the back end is within everyone's reach. One unaltered pair of dogs can produce nearly 4,500 in seven years! From free services offered by vets, city voucher programs, and rescue group programs the population explosion can be controlled, all it takes is a desire to do so.

The homeless problem is not hopeless. There's just a lot that needs to be done. The funny thing about a blessing is that once you create one, it takes on energy of its own and multiplies. Why not create your own Dog Blessings?

The one absolutely unselfish friend
that a man can have
in this selfish world,
the one that never deserts him,
the one that never proves ungrateful
or treacherous, is his dog....
He will kiss the hand that has
no food to offer....
When all other friends desert,
he remains.

— GEORGE G. VEST: SPEECH U.S. SENATE, 1884

BOB LOVKA

Bob Lovka is a Southern California-based writer whose work includes poetry, satire, humor books and calendars, and television, script, and stage show writing. Bob's connection to felines and canines keeps expanding. Homeless cats and dogs look him up constantly, and uncannily they have increased their appearances since Bob wrote *Cat Blessings, The Splendid Little Book of All Things Cat, The Splendid Little Book Of All Things Dog, Cats Rule!, Dogs Rule!, Cats Are Better Than Dogs,* and *Dogs Are Better Than Cats.* Many of these animals have found homes through Bob's association with Angel Puss and Pooch Rescue. Bob is owned by a cat and is tormented by a jealous Lhasa apso.

SETSU BRODERICK

Setsu Broderick's illustrations, decorative designs, and commercial artwork are seen throughout the world. Her whimsical and charming original creations have turned into collectibles, music boxes, plush toys, books, and figurines. She has illustrated *Cat Blessings, The Splendid Little Book of All Things Cat, The Splendid Little Book of All Things Dog, Cats Rule!,* and *Dogs Rule!* Max, her desk-chewing cockatoo, remains her most vocal art critic.